What a Dog's Life!!

20 recipes
to reward your dog

©2010
First printrun April 2010
Author: Manuel Goossens

Joint Publication between Tectum Publishers and Hupple.
For more information:

Tectum Publishers
Godefriduskaai 22
2000 Antwerp
Belgium
info@tectum.be
+ 32 3 226 66 73
www.tectum.be

www.hupple.com

ISBN: 978-90-79761-48-7
WD: 2010/9021/21 (112)

Design: Gunter Segers
Photography: Dieter De Bock

Printed in China.

What a Dog's Life!!

20 recipes to reward your dog

Content

Preface

They sometimes say that the way to a man's heart is through his stomach. This is definitely the case with your dog!

Every day, I rise to the challenge with 'Hupple' to provide the best and most healthy snacks. You could compare it to working in a 'very large kitchen': plenty of dough with carefully chosen ingredients, thousands of baking tins, an incredibly long oven...
Our snacks are truly balanced, made with love and suitable for daily use.

Snacks for dogs should be considered as treats or as a little extra, but definitely not as a meal. They are like the snacks you eat: on special or healthy occasions, they give you an extra boost or reward for the effort you have just made.

All the more reason to start baking yourself! Use your culinary skills for the extra special moments or simply for the rewarding character!

The most tasty and best recipes have been compiled in this book to give your dog the most incredible treats (and you will have fun cooking yourself)!

Enjoy yourself and give your dog a big cuddle!

MANUEL GOOSSENS

Recipes

Your dog needs refreshments when the weather is hot. In addition to water, which is always good, you can give him these (or other) ice lollies. They can be enjoyed as they are, or added to his water bowl to add more flavour and chill to his water!

Fruity Yoghurt Ice Lollies

Perfect in SUMMER or when the weather is WARM.

PREPARATION:
10 minutes + freezing

INGREDIENTS:

- 2 squashed kiwis
- 225 gram strawberry yoghurt (or a different flavour)

Mix everything into a homogeneous paste. Pour into an ice cube tray and freeze.

EXTRA:

Most shops that sell household goods offer funky ice cube trays with different shapes that will add that little extra to the lollies!

Divine Dog Pie

For a FESTIVE occasion

PREPARATION:
10 minutes
+ 90 minutes in the oven

INGREDIENTS:

- 200 grams minced chicken
- 200 grams wheat flour
- 4 dl chicken stock
- bag of mixed vegetables
  (e.g. soup vegetables)
- A few cloves of garlic or
  1 tablespoon garlic powder
- 1 tablespoon olive oil

Blend all ingredients using a food processor or mixer until the paste is smooth, comparable to cake mixture.

Place baking paper in a springform pan and add the paste. Bake the pie in a preheated oven for 90 minutes at 180°C.

EXTRA:

You can decorate the pie afterwards with the left-over vegetables. Candles look great in pictures but be aware: your dog could seriously burn himself!

Heavenly Honey Nibbles

Ideal as TRAINING BISCUITS.

PREPARATION:
10 minutes + 15 minutes in the oven

INGREDIENTS:

- 100 grams flour
- 1 egg
- 1 tablespoon honey
- 5 grams peanut butter
- 60 grams butter
- 1 teaspoon baking powder
- 35 grams oat flakes
- 2 grams vanilla sugar or a few drops of vanilla concentrate.

Honey has a positive effect. For example, it prevents the growth of bacteria such as salmonella, and positively influences intestinal bacterial imbalance (i.e. gastrointestinal tract). Moreover, honey helps to combat cardiovascular diseases and has a relaxing effect. And it tastes good!

Warm up the honey and peanut butter until they are liquid. Use a pan or the microwave, in which case this will take approx. 20 seconds.

Preheat the oven to 175°C. Mix all ingredients together. Grease your baking tray with butter and flour. Spoon the mixture onto the baking tray in small heaps. Bake in the oven for 10 to 15 minutes.

Jingle Balls

Perfect as PARTYSNACK

PREPARATION:
10 minutes + 15 minutes
in the oven

INGREDIENTS:

- 225 grams minced beef
- 1 finely grated carrot
- 1 tablespoon grated cheese
- 1 tablespoon garlic powder
- 1 whisked egg
- 1 tablespoon tomato puree
- 1 cup wholemeal bread crumbs

Preheat your oven to 180°C. Mix all ingredients well and roll them into balls. Place them on a greased baking tray and bake them for 15 minutes in the oven. Wait until they are nicely brown and firm.

Super Vitamin Bombs

For your dog's HEALTH, full of VITAMINS.

PREPARATION:
20 minutes + 15 minutes in the oven

INFO:
Thanks to their tenderness, the biscuits are suitable for puppies and older dogs.

INGREDIENTS:

- 1/4 cup blueberries
- 1 small banana
- 1/2 cup milk
- 2/3 cup oatmeal
- 1/4 cup rye flour

Preheat the oven to 200°C.
Cut the banana into fine slices. Add the blueberries and milk and mix in a blender until smooth.

Pour this mixture into a large bowl and add the oatmeal and rye flour. Mix everything well. Use funky shapes or make balls out of the dough and place them on a greased baking tray.

Bake them for 15 minutes in the oven or until they are brown and crunchy.

EXTRA:

You can replace the milk with soya milk.
If you would rather have hard biscuits, you can leave them in the oven overnight (after you've turned it off of course!)

This snack contains blueberries which are full of nutrients such as manganese, vitamins B6, C and K and important fibres. They are also full of antioxidants which help to prevent illnesses. A different ingredient, the banana, also contains many vitamins and potassium. The porridge and rye flour from the recipe contain a large amount of nutritious minerals.

Poochy Pastry Snacks

Tasty at ANY TIME.

PREPARATION:
**25 minutes + 15 minutes
in the oven**

INGREDIENTS:

- 6 sheets of puff pastry
- 1 tablespoon vegetable oil
- 1 coarsely chopped onion
- Herbs: ginger, mixed green herbs and pepper
- 1 diced tomato without pips
- 1/2 sweet pepper - colour optional
- 1 tablespoon finely chopped black olives
- coarsely chopped parsley leaf
- 3 diced mushrooms
- a few shoots of leek
- bag of grated cheese
- 1/2 litre milk
- small bag of poppy seed

Preheat the oven to 200°C.
Wok the vegetables and herbs.
When they are done, take the pan off the cooker and let the vegetables cool down.

Put some butter on a baking tray and cover with baking paper.

Have the pastry sheets ready. You can now start filling the snacks one by one. Place the stuffing on the pastry and cover with grated cheese. Fold the sheet in two and firmly press the sides. Make two little incisions in the top, brush a little milk on the sheets and cover them with poppy seed.

When they are all ready, place them on the baking tray and in the oven at 200°C. They will be ready in 15 minutes!

Sweet Potato Cakes

**Ideal for dogs
with DIABETES.**

PREPARATION:
**35 minutes
+ 20-30 minutes
in the oven**

INGREDIENTS:

- 1 large sweet potato
- 3 eggs
- 3/4 cup (unsweetened) apple sauce
- 1 tablespoon cinnamon
- 1/2 tablespoon ginger
- 2 cups wholemeal flour
- 1 cup oatmeal
- Different smaller cake tins or one large one

Preheat the oven to 150°C and grease the cake tins.

Wash the sweet potato and prick it several times with a fork. Soften the sweet potato in the microwave. Depending on your microwave, this may take 5 minutes or longer. Start with a few minutes and increase the time if required.

Let the sweet potato cool down, peel it and place it in a large bowl. Using a mixer, blend the sweet potato with the eggs and apple sauce.

In a different bowl, mix the cinnamon, ginger, flour and oatmeal. Create an opening in the middle of this mix and add the sweet potato mixture into it. Firmly stir everything and pour the mixture into the baking tins. Bake for 20-30 minutes in the oven. Leave the cakes to fully cool down.

EXTRA:

These snacks will stay fresh in the fridge for 1 week and up to 3 months in the freezer.

Sweet potatoes are full of nutrients: carbohydrates, fibres, provitamin A, vitamin C and many more. They also help to balance the blood sugar level which makes them into the perfect snack for diabetic dogs.

Ready-to-Chew Chicken Sticks

To train the TEETH and JAWBONE.

PREPARATION:
15 minutes + 20 minutes in the oven

INFO:
Your dog will enjoy this tasty and chewy snack, which is also good for his teeth!

INGREDIENTS:

-   1 chicken filet

Bake the unseasoned chicken filet in the pan until done. Cut it into small strips. Bake these in the oven for 20 minutes at 150°C. Leave them to dry out in the oven for a while.

EXTRA:

Do not be tempted by the longing looks of your dog to finish the strips more quickly. It is best not to bake them at a higher temperature and for a shorter period of time as they will burn. So stick to the recipe!

Frozen Fruitfest

Perfect in SUMMER or when the weather is WARM.

PREPARATION:
10 minutes + freezing

INGREDIENTS:

- 5 pieces of fruit
- 1/2 litre unsweetened fruit juice (pineapple juice is perfect)
- 1/2 litre low fat yoghurt
- honey
- 1/2 tablespoon cinnamon

Blend a mixture of your dog's favourite fruit and add the juice. Use some of the low fat yoghurt to thicken and honey to sweeten the mixture. Season with cinnamon.

Mash everything, pour in small cups and freeze them. Serve them as ice lollies.

EXTRA:

Dogs love fruit such as strawberries, honeydew melon, watermelon, apple, peach and banana. However, tastes differ.

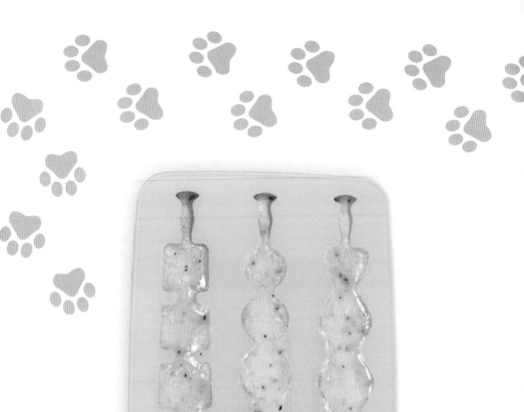

Paradise Pancakes

For a FESTIVE occasion.

PREPARATION:
15 minutes

INGREDIENTS:

- 3 eggs
- approx. 1 packet cream cheese
- 500 grams flour
- 300 grams finely minced meat
- there are several options such as liver, heart and tuna. Choose your dog's favourite.

Mix the eggs, flower and meat together until it is smooth. Now use this to bake pancakes.

Before you serve them, you can spread cream cheese on top. Roll them up and cut them into perfect bite size pieces.

EXTRA:

You can also spread other tasty treats on your dog's pancakes: minced liver, fish or cottage cheese.

MMMMuesli Bars

To SHARE with your dog when out on a WALK.

PREPARATION:
30 minutes + 8 minutes in the oven

INGREDIENTS:

- 1/3 cup olive oil
- 1/4 cup brown sugar
- 1/2 cup peanut butter
- 1 squashed banana
- egg white of 1 egg
- 1 cup wholemeal flour
- 1/8 cup linseed
- 1 tablespoon cinnamon
- 1 1/2 tablespoons baking powder
- 1 3/4 cup oatmeal
- Finely chop 1/8 of each of the following ingredients:
     pumpkin pips
     roasted almonds
     roasted pecans
     roasted peanuts
     dried cranberries
     dried pineapple
     dried banana slices
- 1/8 cup carob (this is a safe replacement for chocolate, which is dangerous for dogs. You can find carob in most health food shops.)

Preheat the oven to 180° C.
Whisk the olive oil and brown
sugar in a large bowl. Add the
peanut butter and mix well. Stir
the banana and egg white into it.
Add the flour, linseed, cinnamon
and baking powder and mix until
smooth. Now add the oatmeal and
stir until it turns into dough.

Mix the pumpkin pips, almonds,
pecans, peanuts, cranberries,
pineapple, banana slices and carob
in a small bowl. Add the fruit mix
to the dough.

Grease a baking tray.
Using your hands, gently shape the
dough into flat biscuits of your
preferred size.

Bake for 8 minutes and let cool
down.

EXTRA:

These biscuits will stay fresh in
the fridge for 2 weeks, and even
up to 4 months in the freezer.

Acidophilus, present in most yoghurt, is a probiotic and has several positive effects: it may improve intestinal flora and the taking in of calcium. This lactic bacterium naturally appears in dairy products, as well as in the bowel. Therefore, yoghurt may be the perfect addition to your dog's diet when he has an upset intestinal flora.

Yummy Yoghurt

Perfect in SUMMER or when the weather is WARM.

PREPARATION:
10 minutes + freezing

INGREDIENTS:

- A large pot of yoghurt with acidophilus and without sugar
- 2 carrots, cut into small slices
- 1 large apple, cut into small pieces
- Cooked pieces of liver

Mix all ingredients together. Scoop the mixture into an ice cube tray or small cups and freeze.

Spectacular Soya Sweets

Ideal solution for dogs with LACTOSE INTOLERANCE.

PREPARATION:
30 minutes + 20 minutes in the oven

INGREDIENTS:

- 1 1/2 cups wholemeal flour
- 1/4 cup porridge
- 1 tablespoon baking powder
- 3/4 cup soya milk
- 3/4 cup peanut butter
- 1 tablespoon honey

A dog becomes lactose intolerant if he does not produce enough lactase, an enzyme which helps to break down lactose. Due to the lack of lactase, the lactose cannot be absorbed in the blood and side effects appear such as nausea, cramps or diarrhoea. Soya milk is a suitable alternative.

Preheat the oven to 180° C. Mix the flour, porridge and baking powder in a large bowl.

Use a blender or mixer to turn the milk, peanut butter and honey into a smooth mix. Add both mixtures together and use your hands to knead it further until the dough is firm and sticky.

Roll the dough out on a surface that is covered in flour to a thickness of approx. 0,5 centimetre. Cut out funky shapes and place them on a non-greased baking tray. Bake for 20 minutes in the oven. Leave the biscuits to cool down overnight in the oven. Ensure that they're entirely cold before you give them to your dog.

Mint leaves smell lovely and fresh. If you squash or chop them up, they will spread their enticing aroma even further. Therefore, they are the ideal treat to make your dog's breath smell lovely. If your dog has bad breath continuously, it is best to take him to the vet. There could be many reasons, which the vet will be able to help out with.

Mouth Refreshing Mint Mates

For a fresh BREATH.

PREPARATION:
40 minutes
+ 30 minutes in the oven
+ 1 hour drying

INGREDIENTS:

- 1 cup corn flour
- 1 tablespoon vegetable oil
- 3/4 cup chicken stock
- 1 egg
- 1 tablespoon grated Cheddar cheese
- 2 tablespoons finely chopped up (fresh!) mint

Preheat the oven to 180° C.
Bring the chicken stock and oil to a boil. Take the pan off the cooker once it has boiled and stir in the corn flour. Pour the mix into a small bowl. Let it cool down until you can touch it. In the meantime, grease a baking tray. When the mix has sufficiently cooled down, add the egg, cheese and mint. Now make little balls or shapes.

Bake the biscuits for 30 minutes. Turn the oven off and leave the biscuits to dry for an hour.

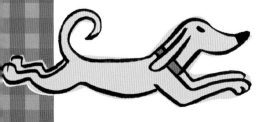

Apple-Cinnamon Biscuits

Ideal as TRAINING BISCUITS.

PREPARATION:
20 minutes + 1 hour in the oven

INGREDIENTS:

- 4 cups wholemeal flour
- 1/2 cup corn flour
- 1 egg
- 2 tablespoons vegetable oil
- 1 small grated apple
- 1 teaspoon cinnamon
- 1 1/3 cup water

Mix the flour, corn flour, egg, oil and cinnamon. Add the grated apple and water. Continue to stir until it becomes a solid mixture. Place it on a surface covered in flour.

Knead the mixture thoroughly and roll it out to a thickness of approx. 1 centimetre. Cut the sheet into 2 x 2 centimetre biscuits.

Place the pieces on a greased baking tray and bake for 1 hour in the oven at 160°C..

TIPS AND TRICKS · BY THE SPECIALIST · TIPS AND TRICKS · BY THE SPECIALIST

When you want to train a puppy, it is best to let him off the lead as much as possible. Practise this in a quiet place such as in woods and always go to a different place. A puppy's instinct is stronger than itself. He knows he cannot survive without you, and will therefore not run away. Whilst you call him, walk in the opposite direction. When your dog follows you, treat him generously with something tasty.

Flavoursome Flea Farewell

Keeps away FLEAS.

PREPARATION:
20 minutes + 20 minutes in the oven

INFO:
Thanks to the yeast in these biscuits, and particularly vitamin B, your dog's blood will be less appealing to fleas. His smell will change and fleas will avoid him. Don't panic, your dog will only smell different to those little pests. You will not notice the difference!

INGREDIENTS:

- 2 cups wholemeal flour
- 1 cup corn flour
- 2/3 cup brewer's yeast
- 2 tablespoons garlic powder
- 2 egg yolks
- 1 1/2 cups boiling water
- 3 stock cubes (beef or chicken stock)

Preheat the oven to 190°C. Dissolve the stock cubes in (warm) water. Mix all ingredients. Add the egg yolks and stock and stir thoroughly. Roll the mixture out on a surface that is covered in flour to a thickness of approx. 1 centimetre. Cut out shapes or slices as desired. Place the biscuits on a baking tray and bake them for 20 minutes in the oven. Leave the biscuits to cool down for at least 3 hours in the oven before you store them in an airtight biscuit tin.

Similar to how garlic manages to keep other people far away from you, it is also extremely efficient in repelling flees. However, it is an ingredient you must not use too often or in large quantities.

Tough Teeth Crunchers

For a FESTIVE occasion.

INGREDIENTS:

- 350 grams flour
- 1 tablespoon cinnamon, nutmeg, cardamom, clove powder and baking powder
- 1 pinch salt
- 250 grams honey
- 2 eggs

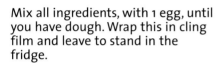

Mix all ingredients, with 1 egg, until you have dough. Wrap this in cling film and leave to stand in the fridge.

After half an hour, roll the dough out on a surface that is covered in flour. Cut out shapes and cover them with a beaten egg. Bake the biscuits in a preheated oven for approx. 15 minutes at 160°C.

Mint is not only tasty but also has a calming effect on dogs, and is a natural antidepressant.

Chirpy Relax Mix

Natural ANTIDEPRESSANT and RELAXANT for dogs.

PREPARATION:
50 minutes + 30 minutes in the oven

INGREDIENTS:

- 2 cups wholemeal flour
- 2/3 cup corn flour
- 1/2 cup sunflower pips
- 1 pinch sugar
- 2 tablespoons corn oil
- 1/2 cup chicken stock
- 2 eggs mixed with 1/4 cup milk
- 1 beaten egg
- 2 tablespoons fresh and squashed mint

Preheat the oven to 180° C.
Mix the flour, corn flour, sugar and pips in a large bowl. Add the oil, chicken stock and milk mix. Leave it to rest for 30 minutes.
Place the mixture on a surface covered in flour and roll it out to a thickness of approx. 1 centimetre. Cut out shapes as desired and cover them all with the beaten egg.
Bake in the oven for 30 minutes until the biscuits are golden brown. Leave them to fully cool down.

Magical Ice Cubes

For a CALMING effect.

PREPARATION:
5 minutes + freezing

INFO:
Lavender is the perfect ingredient to relax your dog. For example, treat him to these tasty ice cubes when he is wound up by visitors. You can let them melt in his water bowl or give him one when the weather is warm.

INGREDIENTS:

- 2 cups water
- finely chopped lavender

Pour the water in an ice cube tray. Add some lavender to every cube. Freeze it.

Seaweed also makes a nice alternative. It will make your dog's coat shiny and healthy. Camomile, on the other hand, is soothing. Ideal when your dog has a painful ailment.

hupple

DINNER IS SERVED

TIPS AND TRICKS · BY THE SPECIALIST ·

It is not always easy to treat your dog to something tasty without it being fatty or meat. This snack is ideal for dogs on a diet!

Very Veggie Crackers

For dogs that have to LOSE WEIGHT.

PREPARATION:
15 minutes + 25 minutes in the oven

INFO:
This tasty vegetable stick is perfect as a health snack. You would like to treat him to something nice without giving him bad things. You can also use the snack during a walk.

INGREDIENTS:

- 1 small courgette
- 1 carrot
- 2 eggs
- 1 tablespoon sunflower oil
- 150 grams wholemeal wheat flour
- 1 to 2 tablespoons milk

Peel the courgette and carrot and grate them. Mix them with the eggs and oil. Add the flour whilst kneading and pour in as much milk as necessary to make good kneadable dough.

Preheat the oven to 175° C.

Place baking paper on the baking tray or grease with butter. Roll the dough into long sticks and place them on the baking tray. Bake for 25 minutes in the oven. Turn the oven off and leave the sticks to dry.

Top tips to preserve

How to store my home-made snacks?

It may be fun making your own snacks for your dog, but it would be sad if you had to throw them all away later. Properly storing all the tasty food allows your hairy friend to enjoy it even longer!

Tin-kle all the way

Home-made dog biscuits need a cool and dry environment. Avoid damp and humid conditions. A pretty biscuit tin helps to keep them longer. And it looks nice too!

Light at the end of the tunnel

Direct sunlight and warmth are the biggest enemies of your delicious snacks. Therefore it is best to store them in a dark place, for example a non-transparent tin.

Freeze please

Your snacks will keep fresh for at least two months if they are stored in an airtight container in the fridge. You can keep them up to eight months in the freezer.

You've won with lemon

Snacks from the shops often contain additives. There are also natural preservatives you could add to your biscuits: vitamin C and E and citric acid (from citrus fruits for example) and rosemary. These are healthy for your dog and help to preserve your cooking.

Crunchy and munchy

The dryness, texture and consistency of your snacks will play an important role. A crunchy or hard biscuit will keep weeks longer than a soft training biscuit or moist snack.

Don't pour oil on the flames

The use-by date of your snacks is largely determined by the ingredients and amount you have used. If you bake biscuits using margarine instead of butter or oil, they can be kept longer.

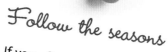

Follow the seasons

If you often take your dog to the market, you can use the opportunity to buy seasonal vegetables and fresh ingredients. This will provide your dog with fresh snacks all year around!

Cool = rule

Ensure that your biscuits have fully cooled down before you store them. Warm biscuits will cause condensation, resulting in mould.

Last but not least: Listen to your dog

Some dogs like their snacks at room temperature. Others love ice cubes and like their nibbles straight from the freezer. Bare this in mind when storing their food.

A few precautions!

Measure your pup's portions:

A few precautions!

As we share our everyday lives with our dogs, we play with them and even tell them our deepest secrets, we sometimes forget that they are dogs. After all, they do have different habits, including their diet.

Therefore, it is important that we take good care when preparing their meals ourselves. Before starting, please read these precautions carefully!

Not everything tasty, is good

The *Top 10 of Don'ts in Your Dog's Diet* further in this book, gives you a good overview of the ingredients that are best to be avoided in your dog's diet. Some of these components are poisonous for your dog, and therefore, are not used in the recipes in this book, or included in the food you buy in the shops. Other ingredients are harmless, as long as they are used in moderation.

Between breakfast and dinner

All the snacks in this book are, as the name suggests, nibbles that can be eaten in between meals. They can be considered as supplements but not as a main course.

A dog's diet should be balanced and you should ensure that only 10% of his energy needs are as a result of supplements such as snacks. The energy needs of each dog are different. You know him best, but if you have questions, you can always consult a specialist or vet.

Give drink to the thirsty

Ensure that, at all times, sufficient drinking water is at hand. It is important that your dog drinks plenty of water at each meal and in between!

Everything in moderation

If you constantly treat your dog to tasty snacks, it is not considered a treat anymore. It becomes a habit. As you do not want to spoil your buddy, only occasionally use the snacks in this cookery book. You will enjoy watching your dog as he waggles his tail with excitement when he sees and smells your culinary delights. To ensure that he continues to find this thrilling, only prepare these recipes on special occasions and include sufficient variety!

If you don't succeed, try try again!

It is important to create habits when you are training your dog. The training biscuits described in this book can be used occasionally, but for long-term training, it is better to buy biscuits from the shop. They are specifically created for this purpose and consist of a balanced composition, which may improve training.

Top 10 of Don'ts in your Dog's Diet

Top 10 of Don'ts in your Dog's Diet

Your dog will be pleasantly surprised with your new hobby! Home-made snacks are more fresh and tastier than those from the shops. However, you have to remember: some ingredients are not always suitable for your pet, and naturally you do not want to make him ill. Therefore, pay attention to the following ingredients. They may have an undesired effect if used in the wrong quantities.

When you treat your dog to a particular snack for the first time, give him a small portion and keep an eye on him for a little while...

Baby Food

Food you feed your child can surely not be bad for your pet? Or can it? Take into account that baby food may contain onions or an excess of sugar and salt. These ingredients should be avoided!

Cheese and Milk

There are people who are lactose intolerant and this is no different with dogs. Small amounts are not dangerous but just keep an eye on him!

Chocolate

Like you, your dog loves chocolate. Try to resist his imploring look when he begs you for a piece of your favourite bar. Except for white chocolate, these sweets are dangerous in dog snacks. It may cause diarrhoea and vomiting, as well as serious conditions such as cardiac arrhythmia, tremor and sometimes fatal heart attacks. There are so many different recipes to try out, so avoid chocolate (and treat yourself to another piece!).

Liver

The distinct and (for your dog) absolutely delicious smell makes it the perfect ingredient to add to training biscuits. Most animals will be on their best behaviour in order to be treated to this yumminess. Be careful though; as with many things, you can have too much of a good thing! Liver that has been cooked for too long may cause vitamin A poisoning. Ensure your dog eats a sufficient variety by changing ingredients often.

Onion

Onions not only make you cry, they may even damage your dog's red blood cells or cause anaemia. Do not use too much onion in your cooking.

Nuts

Macadamia nuts and walnuts must be avoided. They may cause lifelessness and even paralysis. Keep these small dangers out of your dog's reach! Other nuts are safe but are often salty and too greasy. If you like a fit and trim dog: do not feed nuts in excess.

Potatoes

Potatoes are not poisonous for your dog but the green parts are! This is also the case with other members of the nightshade family, such as aubergines, sweet peppers and tomatoes. A small piece of these vegetables will be harmless but pay attention for the green parts.

Raisins and Grapes

We are not sure why, but these seemingly innocent fruits are not healthy for your dog. There is plenty more other tasty fruit, so do not take the risk, just avoid them.

Salt

Why do you add salt to your food? To make it tasty, yes? Dogs have fewer taste buds and instead pick up flavours through their amazing sense of smell. Since salt does not smell, why would you add it to his food? Particularly if you know that it may cause liver problems, or even salt poisoning.

Sugar and Sweeteners

Strange but true: your dog does not even like sugar. This is a good thing because, as with humans, sugar is unnecessary. It causes tooth decay in your dog and he will become fat if he eats too many sweet things. It may also cause his blood levels to fluctuate dangerously.
Be aware: artificial sweeteners are also a no-no.

Notes

Thanks !

Mieke, Inne and Michelle Vangeel
For the fun cooking and baking days in the kitchen of 'Den Moor', a nice quality restaurant in Broechem. Thanks to your creative and professional cookery skills, all the recipes became reality!

The entire Hupple team, with a special thanks to my personal assistant **Steven Huybrechts** and **Dieter De Bock** who supplied mouth-watering photography!